ALL THE DAYS

ALL THE DAYS
Robert Berold

DEEP SOUTH

2008 © Robert Berold
All rights reserved

ISBN: 978-0-9584915-5-6

Deep South
P O Box 6082
Grahamstown 6140
South Africa
www.deepsouth.co.za

Deep South titles are distributed by
University of KwaZulu-Natal Press
www.ukznpress.co.za

Earlier versions of these poems have appeared in :
Aerial, Botsotso, Carapace, Fidelities, Kotaz, New Coin,New Contrast,
Timbila, sweetmagazine.co.za, donga.co.za,
southernrainpoetry.com, litnet.co.za, Mouse and Rattapallax.

Cover painting: *Untitled, 2000* by Tammy Griffin
Text design: Paul Wessels and Katie Wilter
Cover design: Katie Wilter and Robert Berold

Thanks to everyone who helped me put this book together
– especially Joan Berold, Denis Hirson, and Mindy Stanford

Contents

I

The water running	11
Half-light	12
The valley	13
To my room	14
Builders	15
Summer	16
My death	17
Two cats	18
Does it end	19
The light	20
Emergency	22
Journey	23
Beloved	26

II

Things wavering	29
Our Joburg home	30
Joburg zoo	31
Letter to Mary	32
Why I am not an engineer	33
At the wavelength of earth	34
The fire	36
My bakkie	38
The rock thrushes	40
Woman working	41
All the days	42
Night shift Hangzhou	44
Bus stop in the rain	45
The book of changes	46
Woman in China	47
The floor that was never scrubbed	48

III

The invisible poem	51
Writing	52
Invitation	53
Sweetpeas	54
To myself at 20	55
Visit to my mother	56
What I hated	59
Written on my father's birthday	60
Loudness	61
Saxman	62
Love poem with stone	63
Proposal	64
In the thicket of the body	66
The fence	67
On the road	68
Patch of earth	69
The month of may	70

I

The water running

the water running in the gullies
the hoopoe bobbing, flying off abruptly

the sky full of leftover rain
nokwakwa weeding bent straight at the waist

the grass bright green after the fire
the hoopoe in the grass a nervous king

the bakkie loaded up for town
the pipes and ditches swollen with water

the tierhout burnt
the yellowwood burnt

the burnt veld
the water running

Half-light

morning half-light, meeting
two foxes on the farm road,
crossing the railway line, turning
to the white moon,
looking far down to my house,
seeing the lights on.

The valley

> *the valley spirit never dies –*
> *use it, it will never fail*
> *Lao Tsu*

it's we who live here now with the antbears
the porcupines and the bushbuck

the san hunters have been here and gone
the british soldiers been here and gone

the valley's hair spreads out into ferns
her nerves are the underground streams

the mist from the sea passes over her face
her grey eyes see the clouds hurry rain

To my room

When I moved here you were much darker,
so I put in windows and the aerial bookshelf
that runs around above head height. Now
I sleep with a weight of books above me.
I want to cover them, like birds, to keep them quiet.

I've slept three thousand nights in your arms.
You have absorbed my snoring and my dreams.
Your walls have seen dogs, spiders, frogs, snakes too,
and once a porcupine ambled through.

The trees are coming into leaf today.
I tell you this slowly because you've never been outside.

Builders

Emmanuel the disgruntled mason fitted the windows
in a single skin of bricks, which blew down in a heavy wind,
built it up again, cemented in the stones, designed the
  fireplace,
poured the floor – a smooth pond of cement
coloured black with oxide and immaculately floated.

Abraham the nimble carpenter made the gumpole trusses
lifted them onto the walls with apexes hung down,
swung them up, nailed them to the brandering,
nailed on the storm strapping and the corrugated iron
which bangs and rankles as the temperature changes.

Summer

the three-fingered leaves of the rhus tree,
the thick sperm smell of the milkwood.

a mantis disguised as a bent grass.
a spider straitjacketing a bee.

on the road in the headlights
a bushbuck, almost black –

white dots scattered on its flank.

My death

I want to die in bed or sitting on a chair –
like an old car when its axle engine gearbox
all stop working simultaneously.

Stop eating altogether like my dog Max –
say goodbye to friends and enemies
just drink some water to be comfortable.

Here's my will signed and witnessed –
forget about a coffin, use a plank
put me in the ground and plant a celtis tree.

I want above all else to be awake –
I want my fire to burn completely into ash
and if there's anywhere to go I'll be there.

Two cats

to kattekung and hecate

kattekung kattebong
kattekung kattebong
ke-kattekung ke-kattebong
kattebong kung

kung bong kung bong
bingibong kattebong
kattekung kattebong
kattebong kung

king kong bing bong
kitty kitty king kong
kitty kitty katty katty
kattebong kung

kattekung bong
kattebong kung

hecate hecate hecate

Does it end

Does it end with the body
going down into the earth?

Or does it end only when we fade
from the memory of the living?

Do we enter the earth and the air
adding to their frequencies?

And the diaries found under the floor,
do they count as living?

And moments bright
as dust on a winter day?

The light

A boomslang stretches out
to probe a nest. A cloud of birds
surrounds it, frantic.

It slinks across to eat the eggs,
swerves back into the foliage,
cuts the light in two.

    *

A baboon barks on the ridge.
The sun is blind and white,
the sunspots flare and plunge.

In the mountains the radio signal comes
and goes. Scraps of torn cloud glitter.
Light. Sky covering sky. Wind.

    *

The terraces were made many years ago,
cut straight to irrigate lucerne.
You can see their lines on the aerial map.

They are covered with thin blue flowers
that close up when the light goes.
Shreds of flayed clouds colour the sky.

    *

On the highway to Karatara,
on golden wires, the swallows
sit flat folded at the end of day.

At the turnoff to the third gate
the light is so intense
the insects blink.

       *

The light goes down in thick air.
We're alone in the long together
nights and days.

Who can explain
how beauty works, except to say
– here – move over here.

Emergency

Something broke in me, a small tinkling sound,
like one of those red boxes in the train
'In emergency break glass. Boete/Penalty for illegal use R10.'

R10 – it shows how old the sign is.
But I don't want to stop the train,
not if it's travelling towards her.

Journey

With my last strong self
I get on the rasping train
Algoa Express to Joburg,
wake up in Kroonstad
long weeds growing by the track
houses needing paint.
This could be the 1960s
heartbeats fettered and extinguished,
gardens clipped and neat, obsessiveness –
for the ones who kept their heads down.

Vanderbijlpark. People on their way to work.
Bakkies running parallel with the train.
Cosmos flowers pink and white
scattered with bright magenta.

*

*I was waiting in starvation
and starvation found me.*

*If it were only you, you only,
I would wait for you under the eaves,
to fall like rain there.*

*I'm hanging in the sky.
My house is swept.*

*

Hillbrow. Wanderers Street.
Taxi-blasted chickens stand in cages.
I was born here. Florence Nightingale Hospital.
It used to be a dreamy flatland of pensioners
and nurses. The city filled and emptied every day
as orchestrated by the law.

*

> *Across the valley*
> *shadows of the morning sun.*
>
> *You climb upon me*
> *undulating, tidal pull –*
> *a kiss comes from your womb*
> *to touch my tongue.*

*

Dan's face full and crumpled, eyes
creased with old laughter. A truck going
somewhere. I am at Vonani's, drinking tea,
loud traffic in the Polokwane streets.
Is there such a thing as too late?
I think I failed at many things.

*

The NorthLinks bus from Polokwane.
We pass the vendors of holy water
and a handwritten sign that reads
THE HALF-HUMAN RESTAURANT.

We stop in Bela Bela.
Bodies on the front page of The Star.
The Ellis Park stampede, the fans
crushed on the razor wire.

Transvaal Museum, Pretoria.
The fossils of pre-human skulls.
The Roberts Bird Book birds
all stuffed and numbered
standing in sequence in long glass cases.

Fossilised molluscs
200 million years old,
the swirl of our origins,
mud of where we came from,
two hours in a dream.

>   *I have to tell you –*
>   *but from the public phone,*
>   *your answering machine.*

*

6am, near Kommadagga. Almost home.
The train is full. Everybody had a peaceful sleep.
The three guys who were sitting here last night
are having Black Labels for breakfast.

It's been raining in the Eastern Cape.
The rock cuttings glisten in the mist.
Plants cling to the rockface. Acacias
by the track are white with thorns.

Beloved

Love burnt both of us.
Now rain falls in this scorched place.
I lean into your gravity. I will not kill
my love for you. Even if it is
impossible. Even so.

In the fields the stubble is growing.
Rain brushes your face.
A thin moon hangs in the sky,
a piece of brittle cloud.
You walk along the path
your movements unmistakeable.

II

Things wavering

The sun speeds along with the train, through the stands of trees, flickering strobe-light, then quickly sinks. A small station, bushes neatly trimmed. In the smudged dusk, a squatter township, multicoloured shacks. In one yard men sit in blue overalls, drinking.

The newspaper I'm reading says that at any moment, 400 000 people are in the air over Europe. Near-collisions are happening all the time.

The whole station is under a massive rusty iron structure, fluorescent lights embedded in it. In my compartment, half-asleep, I look at the electrical wires overhead, transformer boxes, glass insulators, concrete cylinders of silos. Behind them a few big pine trees.

Once when I was driving down the farm road with a bakkie-load of bricks, a lynx flashed across. I saw its tufted ears up close. Its fur was red as an Irish setter.

Our Joburg home

I have been sitting in the cockpit of my brain, my body lumbering on behind.

I've assembled my writing, my porcupine quills, my photographs, even the life that shimmers through my body. I think of my friend the violinist, who had the courage to busk for money in the street.

I carried my bag all this way. I hear my father's voice saying *No use to man or beast*. I pick up my double bass and carry it, my dog Max walking behind me. That is the extent of my performance.

The angels speak, the dogs speak, the trees speak, languages we cannot hear. And Ike and Isabella sing – "money here, money there, for hard times, a cool drink, our home on a rock, our Joburg home".

The wall divided that room from the other room, that other house, the neighbours with their lamps. I wanted all the walls to fall down like the wall of Jericho.

Joburg zoo

The same parking lot I crossed as a boy, the same forest of Forest Town, only the trees are much bigger now. The same seal swimming pool ('that suns his puckered back, that barks from Pirus rock'). And in the cage of the polar bear, who used to pad forever lonely up and down, there's now a Snowy Owl from North America. A bearded monkey from Sumatra and a tiny Suni buck from Kenya share a patch of winter sun. A teenage chimpanzee, pained from being peered at, holds a cardboard box over his head. In the reptile house, in a glass box warmed by high-watt lights, an African bullfrog, fat as a cowpat, blinks from his puddle. Near the elephants, a notice on a tree lists animal life expectancies, in captivity and in the wild: Homo Sapiens is listed as in captivity.

Letter to Mary

I tried to get to see your grandchildren. I phoned the only shop at Sepanaphudi. A manual operator put me through. I asked him if he knew the Theleles. Yes, he said, they're all here, who do you want to speak to?

I phoned the next day, spoke to one of them. Didn't get his name but he knew mine. Mr Robert? – Come and see us quickly. Bring clothes, girls' clothes, and food. We are all without job. Can you come tomorrow? Put off by his desperation, I didn't go.

I'll still come one of these days and visit your grave. Long ago you carried me from the noise into the sunlight. How much I've tried to pay my debt to you. Only to find that debts of guilt are endless. And debts of love? There are no debts of love.

Why I am not an engineer

thanks frank o'hara

I am not an engineer. but I studied
to be one. those days, the 60s, we
went to varsity in shorts and long socks and
threw paper aeroplanes in class. chem.eng.
was a tough course. the theoreticians did well
but the real engineers, the guys who drank beers
and fixed their own cars, failed.
                                              we did a lot of maths
and a lot of chemistry, then in 3rd year the maths
mated with the chemistry, generating monstrous equations,
which we had to solve.
                         what was insoluble was when
they took our class to modderfontein and sasolburg.
dressed in white coats and plastic hats we looked at miles
of hissing pipes and bulging orange flames.
                                        so I became a writer.
no, I first became confused.
                            I remember the day I fainted.
I thought "I join the universe!" my knees gave way.
my head hit the concrete floor. my being
took off with heavy flapping into a sky
which kept on moving through another sky.

At the wavelength of earth

The lights go out in the cities
one by one as the scores are settled.
The vests of sunbirds glint
– if only the light would come down.
The venom of adders concentrates
over thousands, millions, of years.

My soul was eaten first by dogs, with red tongues
and black lips. Then came distorted birds
with mandibles and talons. Then human being-like
creatures came, their energies thickened by desire.
Until the rivers washed me clean and floated me
down cobble beds and riffle zones.

I would like to go back down into the rocks
and become the forest. I would like to move
positively on the airwaves, in the lightbulbs
and aerial connections. I would like a last reminder
that our minds are only partially our own,
that we come from a more luminous continuum.

I would like Jesus to come down and demonstrate,
on live TV, that kindness is a more efficient way to live.
then put a kink in every gun to render it inoperable,
then perform the real miracle: prune human appetites
so none of us want more than what we need
of food and work and pleasure and community.

The mind after death is nine times sharper
says the Tibetan Book of the Dead, but we live here
where memory has a destination, where thousands
of things scurry around, pass messages, eat
each other, in steady cycles of decay and beauty.
This is our place, the economics we return to.

The word comes out of the ground at the wavelength of earth,
it shocks the human heartbeat into starting.
The word comes out at the scale of the soil
a pure sound the frequency of bacteria.
It spreads out far into the sky
with the brilliant yellow of the future.

The fire

The fire started in our valley, in the middle of the bush. How, we don't know. Someone walking through with a cigarette, or the sun magnified through a broken bottle.

We smelled it before we saw it, about noon on a very hot December Saturday, a big white mass of smoke above the trees on the south side of the valley, driven by strong wind.

By the time we got there it had already crossed the road, heading into the alien trees – wattles and pines – crashing, cackling, flaming four metres high.

The fire brigade arrived in one little red 4x4. They watched helpless as flames roared through the aliens, huge tongues of white and brown smoke, a thickly acrid smell, a radiant heat that burnt our skin from twenty metres.

There were only six of us, hitting the flames with firebeaters, big rubber flyswatters. We ran back and forth, the grass was dry and burning everywhere.

Exhausted, eyebrows singed, arms burnt, overwhelmed by smoke and heat and running, I had to sit down for 15 minutes and just watch the fire run away from me.

We carried on fighting that day, and the next day. It spread to the next two farms. Our neighbour took his papers and his domestic animals, and left. He sent SMSs to his church friends. He and his house were saved by prayer, that's what he said.

It took four days for the fire to burn out completely. Field mice arrived on our lawn, half-dead. One of us picked up a small buck, just sitting in the grass, confused. One of the giant mountain tortoises, 70 years or more, was burnt black. Who knows what snakes and insects. That night on our telephone we found a baby mouse, completely still.

My bakkie

1984 was a big year for me. Wally and I started the Power Station, I went to fetch Max as a puppy from Bennie Strydom's farm, my first book was published, and I bought my bakkie. My own brand new Toyota Hilux 2.0 long-wheelbase smooth-running bakkie costing R10 000, its strange canopy with square bumps like a medieval castle.

I drove it every day from Cross Street to the Power Station, drove it to Joburg on our first sales trip selling wooden toys, drove it to Cape Town, to Durban, to the Kruger Park to sell crafts to the buyer in Skukuza, to Joburg again many times, to the township hundreds of times. I lent it to people I trusted and people I didn't trust, people with and without drivers' licences.

I drove with tears in my eyes, Max by my side, camping in the bakkie with Patricia at Dwesa, watching the eland on the beach, knowing glumly that this was the end of us together. A month later my bakkie was crashed into by a police van in George Street while Patricia was moving her stuff. The passenger door was stoved in almost up to the gear lever. I had to drive it with no windscreen to Pretoria to have its body straightened out at the Toyota factory in Silverton.

I let the guys on the farm drive it. One day they dared Nceba, the youngest, to drive while it was loaded full of stones, and he overturned it. The roof had to be pushed back into shape by Alfredo the panelbeater with a hydraulic jack. I got my VW beetle, Max died, my bakkie started losing power on the hills. I demoted it to farm work only.

A few years later while I was far away, in another country, Nceba convinced Johann that his pregnant wife was unable to walk up the hill, and Johann lent him my bakkie. Nceba crashed into a cow or a tree depending on whose story you believe. The bonnet was completely buckled. I had to decide whether to scrap the bakkie or to repair it properly, and I had it repaired, using the money from the UN job. It was promoted back to being my own. I didn't lend it to anyone anymore.

One summer evening I came back with the groceries and parked on the slope outside my house. As I switched on the kettle I saw my bakkie rolling down the hill. I shouted to it "Hey! Where the fuck you going?" but it didn't listen, just carried on rolling over the veld, demolishing a fence post, crashing slowly into one of the big logs anchoring the nursery.

On the fourth day of the Grahamstown Festival, July 2003, on the way home to the farm, the clock turned over 300 000 km. I stopped right there. It was just me and my bakkie, the sunset and the dust road.

The rock thrushes

The rock thrushes have two sounds, an aggressive warning of loud clicks, and a whistling song. The song, sung by the male, has fixed notes and rhythms, then he improvises at the end. I whistle the rock thrush song to them and they check me out with their 270-degree vision. They sing every day, even in the rain.

I love their plumpness and their boldness. Whenever they can, they come into the house, especially the female. Not fazed by my moving around, she hops two-legged along the wooden beam to get a better look at me. And then she flies out confidently, through the open door.

This is the third generation of rock thrushes since I've been here. The first male was a serious musician, with complex improvisations. The second hardly whistled at all. This one is more of a pop singer, not straying from the theme tune, and louder than the others.

My cat got some of the second generation, but these ones are sharp. The male is a brighter colour than the previous ones, his chest a redder rust, his slate blue head more blue. The female dives down to steal a catfood pellet from the bowl.

Woman working

she is working at her computer
on a swivel chair inside a tiny
rondavel which used to be a silo.

the sky is reflected in the screen
her hand is on her left-handed mouse.
concentration grips her toes.

points of her compass:
son, money, friends, her lover (me),
her dog at the doorstep, grey at the whiskers.

she frowns darkly over her hair
which is not dark at all but straw-coloured
with grey in it. colours stream in around her:

the thick kikuyu green, almost unnatural,
the dark and light greens stretching up the valley
grey slabs of cliff, soil pinky-brown after the rain.

All the days

Still autumn day, horizon on all sides,
the old dog snoring in the sun. Butter-yellow
sunlight illuminates a honeysuckle shrub
in which a furtive shrike half-scuttles.

                                       The bell rings
it's Zanemvula, he wants something to eat, he's sick
and thin, not functioning in his fear-filled world.
Blue card, he says, he wants his unemployment card.
I say: There are no more blue cards, they use computers now.
I give him bread with Black Cat peanut butter, and two oranges.

                Zwelinzima's digging out the telephone poles,
they've had their day, the signal goes by microwave now
because of all the theft of copper wire. The poles
look strange lying horizontal by the road, their white
ceramic insulators like tumours.

                            I've just caught up
several months of debt, and I'm driving to town,
with spring water and vegetables, in my one-eyed bakkie –
its headlamp fell out on the shaky road the other night.
It will be repaired on Monday when the part arrives from PE.

                                        In August
I'm going to China, to live among a thousand million people.
Who will take care of Mindy? Who will take care of my cat?
Who will take care of all the days that pass through here?

                                  The phone rings,
it's a wrong number, a text message converted electronically

into a male computer voice which says:
"I'm sending this from my mom's phone.
I miss you very very much. Maria.
I'm sending this from my mom's phone.
I miss you very very much. Maria."
                    I think of Maria.
I think of the wind carrying silence and autumn light.

Night shift Hangzhou

Down, down, below zero, and the wind biting,
I am almost falling asleep on my feet. I imagine
summer in South Africa, sizzling with electric fences.
What is an electric fence? asks Zheng Wei.
I'm waiting for my evening class. I need to sleep. My dinner,
rice and beef soup, metabolises into waking dreams.

I look out over the gleaming polished floors of Building 6,
past Building 5, over the artificial lake, beyond the last farmers' fields,
the ones the university hasn't yet expropriated. In the
pollution-heavy sunset, from the scaffold-clad construction sites,
stutterings of brilliant flashes on the 8th floor and the 12th floor,
pinpoints of arc welding – peasant-workers on the night shift.

Bus stop in the rain

the wet queue moves forward –
that's enough! shouts the driver – *is this when
you say 'packed like sardines'?* asks lan tian.

I think of silvery sardines in a silver tin –
at least we have our heads and tails.
what's that word ending with szze?

the bus surges through the puddles –
umbrellas float above the pavements
bubbles in a moving stream.

where's this bus going? *not sure*
why don't you ask this lady? – *ok –
she says it's going in the right direction.*

The book of changes

the book I couldn't believe
book older than the bible

that came into my life by accident
that told me there were no accidents

book that explained male and female
unfinished book of keys and riddles

book I kept when I sold all my books
book next to which a very small bird landed

the book that proved that poetry was practical
the book that helped me leave home

book that befriended me
book that I store horizontal

the book I carry on my travels
the last book I will ever need

Woman in China

excited by the newness of everything
she takes photos with her new canon powershot
she dresses in her shiny brown silk zip-up top
she composes long indelible poems
she has the oldest cellphone in china
anxiety in her furrowed brow, she takes a picture
she waves to the children who call out 'teacher mindy!'
she studies chinese characters and forgets them
she notices the chinese women's long torsos
she wonders if the disposable chopsticks have been recycled
she has the classic-shaped mouth of a beauty
she's a queen at 50 and thicker at the waist
heat and mosquitoes come in through the porous window

The floor that was never scrubbed

the cockroaches hiding there
except for the one that I stood on
barefoot in the dark bathroom

and now the other one comes
looking for its mate
antennae twitching

III

The invisible poem

the invisible poem pre-exists
so that the reader reading thinks
"but that's what I was thinking all along"

the poem anonymous on the fridge door
like a tree that doesn't know who planted it
and the reader's voice saying "that's exactly"

Writing

I was seven or so, we had handwriting as a subject,
we took our pencils and wrote sentences dictated by
the kind Miss Dunn who wrote the date upon the board

in pale blue chalk. My writing was correct and perfect,
running on invisible tramlines, not a hint of flow in it.
It was the 50s, Johannesburg still had trams, am I that old?

How could it be that her voice travelled into my ears
down my arm and fingers to my pencil, and back again
to my eyes, and somehow, even, to my ears? How could it be?

Invitation

I was invited to my old school. I took
a handful of my own and other people's poems.
I said to them: Each education uses
several tons of paper, and my tons
cremate into these flickering pages.
I said: see how the crevice of your elbow
disappears when you straighten out your arm.

Sweetpeas

I'm the oldest, so I get the cowboy suit and gun.
Derek gets the Indian headdress and the bow and arrow.
Grant, who's 3, gets something only vaguely Indian, a feather.
Here we are in black and white in my mother's Brownie camera.

These days Derek and Grant are wealthy men.
They don't look like Indians at all, nor are they slender.
And I'm no cowboy, though there were some stray cows
near my house on Saturday (I phoned the neighbour).

Nor is there any of the sweet and awkward closeness
that you see between us. But that's me, 50 years ago,
standing there so shy. And that's that part of the garden,
definitely – the wall, the wire frame where the sweetpeas grew.

To myself at 20

I think of myself in Ingrid's bedroom,
under that poster of Bonnie and Clyde
with dark rings under my eyes,
while her mother wept continuously
and her brother muttered threats.

My shield made out of poetry, each line
sonorous and shining, to flash in the dark mine
I was trapped in. Taking the bus to that vacation job
in the Epic peanut butter factory, walking down Loveday Street
reciting Pound's 4th Canto: "Palace in smoky light…"

To escape, escape, but not knowing from what –
so many fears and trying to outrun them,
speeding in my mother's car at 3am
on Ontdekkers Road, playing a game with death
that didn't even frighten me but frightens me today.

Visit to my mother

The pink and red Impatiens in her garden
look artificial. And the lawn too green. But all
of Rosebank and its malls look artificial to me.
I feel stranded among her fish forks and knives.
The family photos have congealed inside their frames.

"Do you believe in evolution?" she asks. "That's a fact,"
I say, "it's not a matter of belief." She doesn't like the fact
that humans started off in Africa. "What about
the different races? And the different cultures? How
can they work these things out from a pile of old skulls?"

"The Sunday Times has a black editor, hasn't it?"
"Yes," I say. "That's why it's full of sex" she says.
"It's always been," I say, "and anyway
those stories come from British newspapers."
"It's even more these days," she says,

"that's all they're interested in – sex and thieving."
Her racism is savage as ever.
I've come to see her because she's been ill.
In intensive care. She could have died.
"They all pinch" she says.

"Last month they pinched a car
from the parking garage." Pinch – that's the word
she uses. She seems quite healthy now
except she has a pinched nerve in her spine,
she has to use a wheelchair or a walking frame.

"Do you believe in reincarnation?" she asks.
She's 86. "I believe in everything," I say.
"Well I don't," she says. "I've been so weary recently,
so old, so tired. I do believe in God, though.
I don't know why, because I'm cynical. Do you?"

"Believe in God? Sure, but I prefer the Dao.
Less anthropomorphic." "Less what?" The TV is on
much too loud. "I have no talent," she says "I've never had
a talent."
"You've always been bright. And you're still alert," I say,
"surely you have some redeeming qualities?"

"A sense of humour," she says "it's helped me stay around
this long. And I like having happy people round me."
Maki, her live-in nurse, seems happy (and she doesn't pinch).
My mother's hair is getting thin. "God," I think, "I'm almost 60,
my hair is white too, and most of it is gone." I think to myself:

"59 years ago I was in this woman's womb."
Her soup spoon clatters in her plate.
"Well I'll be gone soon, to the next world,
and none of you will miss me". My youngest
brother Grant arrives, he's visiting her as well.

"Why did you go into psychotherapy?" he asks me.
We'd started talking about this yesterday
when he fetched me from the airport. My mother answers
"Therapy is when you pay a lot of money to someone
to tell you that you had bad parents."

"Things were a mess for me," I tell him. "My life just wasn't working." "But couldn't you work out your problems and then leave them behind?" "Yes" my mother says, "we all had to get on with it." "Maybe for you" I say to him, "but for me the story had to be untangled first. It took a lot of time."

Next day she says "You're right, I was
a bad mother. I was too anxious. I apologise."
"That's OK," I say. "I accept your apology."
"I go down on my bended knees," she says.
"Don't ruin it with sarcasm," I reply.

A meeting with her accountants. Her finances are healthy.
Her car needs a service. She can't drive anymore but
it's there for her three sons when we visit her in Joburg.
"You can't stop worrying about your chirrun," she says.
That's the way she says it. Chirrun. I kiss her on the head goodbye.

What I hated

what I hated
was the way they used to laugh

the way pain and confusion
was funny to them

the way they would ask questions
and laugh at your answer

what are you looking at? nothing
you calling me nothing?

they way they spoke about beating up kaffirs
what had kaffirs ever done to them or me?

the way I was torn between wanting to be part of them
and wanting nothing to do with them

and if I wasn't part of them
what was I part of?

Written on my father's birthday

I sometimes wonder about my father,
the army major who was once a ballroom dancer.
I wonder about the music that he danced to,
or what music he would play to calm his nerves.

he used to make pronouncements over dinner
such as "never take advice from a woman".
my father built a solid house for us
and there we lived for 27 years.

he used to say "religion is just mumbo-jumbo".
I sometimes wonder how he felt after his death.
he wasn't lonely enough to come back as a ghost
or present enough to touch me with the current of his being.

Loudness

tension builds tightening
the hamstrings winding them
like elastic-powered planes
nerves sizzle and
the gas burns blue
a heat so hot the oil smokes
the washing machine explodes
every sound is too loud
a clink of fork on plate
every word has burnt away

Saxman

with his boy's face and his red cheeks
he's working, blustering, blasting, farting,
cooking his way through a bravado solo,
sax a small reed in his hands,
sweat dripping off him, eyes bulging,
stomach heaving, one with his breath,
lifted from his mother's rasping voice,
his enormous hunger, his domestic burdens,
he veers into a lyrical aside, a laughing reggae riff,
and enters the black heaven he's excluded from.

Love poem with stone

my heart is blocked
there's a big rock or stone
that I must push
and whether it is
my stone or your stone
it's a stone and a big one
and what I want to ask you is
please will you help me push it
push it out the way

Proposal

I'm becoming an extension of my computer.
my fingers are stiff from the keys. and it's not like
I'm a concert pianist or even a concert poet.

I'm reading a book called 'say no to arthritis'
the fact is that my bones are croaking a yes .
the doctor says I should just stop eating bread.

I read in the gospel of mary (oh yes, it does exist, in coptic,
translated willis barnstone) that sin is loving what deceives you.
as in: don't eat today's bread, it has everything milled out of it,

so that it just turns into sugar on the tongue. still, I'm lucky.
our taps have spring water in them. I have a happy doctor.
and a beautiful wife to be, though she makes toast in the morning.

I'm wired up to the world. I can communicate with china, it's only
a six hour time difference. it's the cultural difference
that makes it difficult. and the fact that their rivers are toxic:

some rivers there don't even reach the sea.
living like that, according to the gospel of mary, is a sin.
on the other hand, they have no bread, or very little, it's all rice.

I'm about to get married to mindy stanford. it's a sinless act.
we are both over 50. we have an ante-nuptial contract.
but what about the post-nuptial contract? or any other

marital, nuptial, connubial, matrimonial contracts?
according to her I am married already to my house on the farm,
to my computer (at least email) and to my cat. and I am,

so it's a polymorphous situation. mindy stanford,
please be my wife! let us be uxurious and luxurious!
I want to be married to you for better or for worse, for good.

In the thicket of the body

in the thicket of the body, along one capillary
the pulse moves in its daily circuits round the lake,
cells fire against cells, the liver hurts the liver.

in the thicket of the body, between
the branches, a shiver of wings, a bird
recovering after a long flight, or dying quietly.

The fence

Another fence to keep the Xhosas out,
look how it strides around the property.

Its barbed wire rusted, no longer electrified,
its steel poles stranded here forever.

But in its day, with high voltage and dogs,
this fence defeated everything.

On the road

a man on the road with a load of charred firewood on his back. a bakkie stops and offers him a lift.

a woman on the same road with a bundle of brooms on her head. the brooms are bright green, cut from a stiff shrub.

a woman sweeping her yard with a small switch, back straight, bent low at the waist. there are threadbare chickens walking around, and two blue plastic buckets outside. she hums with the radio. in the kitchen is a tin with mealie meal, a packet of sugar, a packet of teabags.

a hired bus carrying a soccer team, young warriors singing loudly.

a man with TB struggling to breathe.

a sick girl with a yellow jersey who knows she is going to die, skipping as she walks. the trees bend a little to greet her.

Patch of earth

when I think of the people who died
especially the ones who died young, like peter ruffel

I want to say their names aloud –
here in earth time I remember you

when I think of the chances of being born –
one drop in the ocean's chance, say the buddhists

I know that all is well on this patch of earth
on this still and perfect day of autumn

with water in my taps, a roof that doesn't leak
and nobody coercing me into anything

The month of may

may is the month for me. by then
the summer has burnt itself out,
the winter has begun to bite, the days
are still long, and I can practise being
an old man who watches the sun go down,
the stillness and weight of the air
deep as lagoon water layered with colour,
the nights cold enough to drive me
into human company, laughter
from two doors away, and a truck
going past, with airbrakes wheezing,
for a short while there's that field of
child-time, haystacks of time to play in,
and I stay until the lights remind me to go in.

www.ingramcontent.com/pod-product-compliance
Lightning Source LLC
Chambersburg PA
CBHW050918160426
43194CB00011B/2457